WE COME FROM

Jamaica

ALISON BROWNLIE

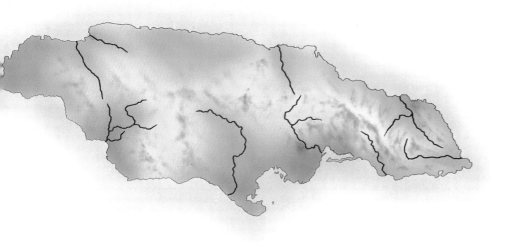

RSVP

RAINTREE
STECK-VAUGHN
PUBLISHERS
A Steck Vaughn Company

Austin, Texas

WE COME FROM

Brazil • China • France
Germany • India • Jamaica • Japan
Kenya • Nigeria • South Africa

The people you are about to meet live in a town in Jamaica called Spanish Town. Like any other country, Jamaica has many different lifestyles. People live in the country as well as in towns and cities.

Cover: Jo-Ann and Kyle with one of their friends

Title page top to bottom: The beach at Montego Bay; a tourist guide with a tropical flower; a street in Kingston; a worker on a banana plantation; a bauxite mine near Mandeville

Contents page: Boys practice their soccer skills.

Index: Jo-Ann waves good-bye.

© Copyright 2000, text, Steck-Vaughn Company

Published by Raintree Steck-Vaughn Publishers, an imprint of Steck-Vaughn Company

Printed in Italy. Bound in the United States.
1 2 3 4 5 6 7 8 9 0 03 02 01 00 99

Library of Congress Cataloging-in-Publication Data
Brownlie, Alison.
Jamaica / Alison Brownlie.
    p.   cm.—(We come from)
    Includes bibliographical references and index.
    Summary: Introduces the land, climate, people, and culture of Jamaica.
    ISBN 0-8172-5511-7
    1. Jamaica—Juvenile literature.
    [1. Jamaica.]
    I. Title. II. Series.
    F1868.2.B76   1999
    972.92—dc21   98-52970

Picture Acknowledgments: Alison Brownlie 10 (bottom), 20 (bottom); Eye Ubiquitous/David Cumming 14 (bottom); John Wright 17 (top). All the other photographs in this book were taken by Howard Davies. The map artwork on the title page and page 5 is by Peter Bull.

Contents

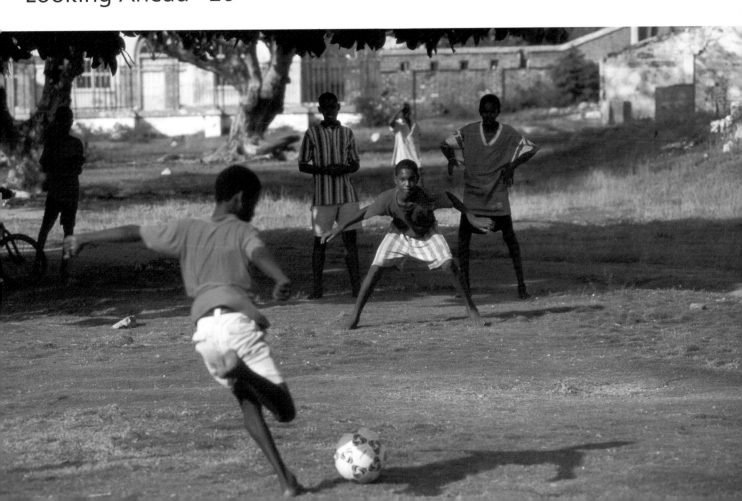

Welcome to Jamaica!

"My name is Jo-Ann. Here I am with my mother and father and my little brother, Kyle, who is six."

Jo-Ann Johnson is eight years old. She lives with her family in Leiba Gardens, a suburb of Spanish Town. Spanish Town is the third largest town in Jamaica, after Kingston and Montego Bay. You can see where all these towns are on the map on page 5.

▲ From left to right: Mr. Johnson, Kyle, Jo-Ann, and Mrs. Johnson.

► *Jamaica's place in the world*

▼ *Jamaica is an island in the Caribbean Sea.*

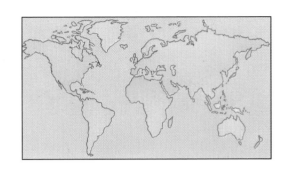

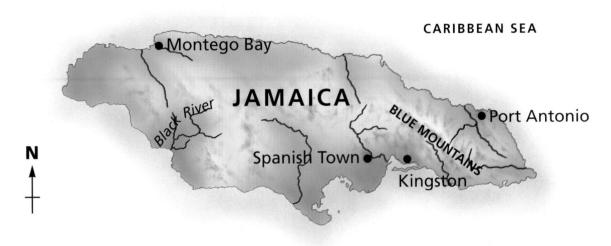

CARIBBEAN SEA

Montego Bay

JAMAICA

Black River

BLUE MOUNTAINS

Port Antonio

Spanish Town

Kingston

N

JAMAICA CHANNEL

| 0 | | 50 km |
| 0 | 20 miles | |

MORANT CAYS

PEDRO CAYS

JAMAICA

Capital city:	Kingston
Land area:	4,217 sq. mi. (11,000 sq. km)
Population:	2.5 million people
Main language:	English
Main religion:	Christianity

The Land and Weather

Most of Jamaica is hilly, and in some places the land is too steep to grow crops. Around Spanish Town, where Jo-Ann lives, it is much flatter. Farmers grow sugarcane in the countryside around the town.

► *Tourists take boat trips along the Black River.*

▼ *This ferry carries passengers across Kingston Harbor. It is one of the biggest harbors in the world.*

► *Some parts of the island are covered with thick, green forests.*

7

◀ These are coffee beans. The weather in Jamaica is good for growing coffee.

It is hot in Jamaica all year round. Sometimes there is heavy rain, which can cause flooding. It rains more often in the north of the island than it does in the south. The rain helps plants grow, so the northern part of Jamaica looks very green.

▼ Parts of this house sank into the ground after an earthquake in 1907.

"We have a lot of sunshine in Jamaica, but we also have big storms and sometimes even hurricanes." — Kyle

9

At Home

Most people in Jamaica live in houses rather than apartments. In the country, houses are usually quite small. They have wooden walls, and the roofs are made of corrugated metal. Since the weather is warm all year round, people spend most of their time outside.

▼ *People sometimes build their own houses. This one is near Port Antonio.*

▲ *Jo-Ann and Kyle spend a lot of time playing in their yard.*

▶ *These luxury houses are in Red Hills, a suburb of Kingston.*

11

► *Kingston is a busy city with tall office buildings and hotels.*

▼ *Jo-Ann's family can afford to have television and a microwave oven.*

Many people have moved to the towns to find jobs. The poorest people live in shantytowns on the edges of Kingston and Spanish Town. Wealthier people, like Jo-Ann's family, live in the suburbs.

"In our new house I will have my own bedroom where I can keep all my books."—Jo-Ann

Jo-Ann's house is small, so she has to share a room with her brother, Kyle. Soon the family is going to move to a new house, and everyone will have more space.

Jamaican Food

Jamaicans like food that is spicy and peppery. Jerk chicken is a special dish, cooked over a wood fire. The national dish is salt fish and ackee. Many different kinds of fish are caught in the sea around the island.

▼ *Jerk chicken is often cooked and sold by the roadside.*

▲ *Ackee is a fruit. It can give off a poisonous gas when it is opened.*

14

"I like sandwiches, but my favorite meal is rice, peas, and chicken."—Jo-Ann

15

Long hours of sunshine and heavy rain help crops grow well in Jamaica. People who live in the country often grow their own fruit and vegetables.

▲ *Bananas are kept in plastic bags while they are growing, to keep insects out.*

"I chop open the coconuts so people can taste the coconut milk—it's delicious and very good for you!"—Market trader

▲ *At the market, people sell the fruits and vegetables they have grown.*

In the towns, people buy food from market stands, as well as from modern shopping malls. Yams, breadfruit, coconuts, plantain, and mangoes are favorite foods.

At Work

In the country, many people work on plantations. They grow foods such as pineapples and bananas, which are sold to other countries.

Many Jamaicans work in hotels, looking after people who come to the island on vacation. Jo-Ann's mother works for the Jamaica Tourist Board in Kingston.

▲ *This Rastafarian man sells souvenirs to tourists.*

▼ *Bananas are washed and packed into boxes. Then they are loaded onto ships.*

"I like meeting people from different countries. I am very proud of Jamaica."—Beverley Johnson, Jo-Ann's mother

At School

All children up to the age of 11 go to school. Then, if they pass an exam, they can go on to secondary school. Some children do not go to secondary school because their parents cannot afford it.

▲ *All schoolchildren have to wear a school uniform.*

▶ *These children have some of their work displayed on the classroom wall.*

◀ *A school for Rastafarian children*

21

▲ *Jo-Ann's teacher helps her at the chalkboard.*

School starts early in the morning, when it is still cool. It finishes around half-past one in the afternoon. Jamaican children have to do a lot of homework after school.

◄ *A girl gets ready to serve the ball in a school volleyball match.*

Jo-Ann's favorite subjects are English, math, and religious education. She is learning Spanish too, which she thinks is fun, but hard work. Sometimes she works on the computer—nearly all schools in Jamaica have them.

"I enjoy reading stories about Robin Hood. Sometimes I read them out loud for Kyle."—Jo-Ann

Free Time

Sports such as soccer, baseball, and basketball are very popular. In towns and cities, people often join sports clubs and youth clubs. Children in the country play games anywhere they can.

On weekends families like to spend time together. Both adults and children enjoy watching television.

▲ Some families go to church together on Sundays.

► These boys are enjoying a game of basketball.

"I go to Brownies every Thursday. All my friends go, too. We have a great time!"—Jo-Ann

Looking Ahead

Jamaica is a beautiful and lively country. People enjoy going there on vacation, and tourism provides jobs for Jamaicans. But some people are afraid that the island will be spoiled if too many hotels are built.

▼ *Jamaica's beaches may be spoiled if too many people come here.*

▲ *Luxury yachts in Kingston Harbor*

"When I am older, I would like to work in the tourist industry, like my mother."—Jo-Ann

Sky Juice Recipe

Sky juice is made from fruits that grow all over Jamaica.

Ingredients

6 Oranges

1 Grapefruit

1 can pineapple chunks

Ice cubes

Equipment

2 Tall glasses

Knife

Lemon squeezer

Pitcher

Rolling pin

▲ *Jo-Ann squeezes an orange.*

1. Slice the grapefruit and oranges in half and squeeze out the juice into the pitcher.

2. Wrap the ice cubes in a towel and crush them with the rolling pin.

3. Put the crushed ice in the glasses.

4. Pour in the juice, add the pineapple pieces and enjoy a cool drink with your friends.

▶ *Jo-Ann and Kyle enjoy a refreshing drink of sky juice.*

Jamaica Fact File

Money Facts
Jamaican money is the Jamaican dollar. There are 100 cents in one dollar. One Jamaican dollar is about the same as 40 cents.

Sports
Merlene Ottey is a Jamaican runner who has won Olympic gold medals. The Jamaican soccer team became famous in 1998 when it reached the final rounds of the World Cup for the first time.

Highest Peak
Jamaica's highest ▶ mountain is called the Blue Mountain Peak. It is 7,402 ft. (2,256 m) high.

The Jamaican Motto
The motto is, Out of many, one people. Jamaican people's ancestors came from many different places, including Africa, Europe, and Southeast Asia. Now they are all Jamaicans.

Longest River
▼ Jamaica's longest river is the Black River, which is 14 mi. (22.5 km) long. It is home to the Jamaican crocodile.

The Jamaican Flag
◀ Each of the colors on the Jamaican flag has a special meaning—green for the land, yellow for the sun, and black for the people.

Famous Jamaicans
The reggae ▶ musician Bob Marley was a very famous Jamaican. He died in 1981. Marcus Garvey was a Jamaican who worked hard to make Jamaica free and independent.

Glossary

Corrugated metal Thin, wavy sheets of metal.

Harbors Places where ships and boats can be loaded and unloaded.

Plantations Large farms where crops are grown to be sold to other countries.

Rastafarian Someone who believes Haile Selassie, who was emperor of Ethiopia, is a god.

Reggae A type of music that developed in the Caribbean. It is now popular in many countries.

Shantytowns Areas of very poor houses on the edge of a large town or city.

Souvenirs Things that people buy to remind them of a place they have visited.

Suburb An area of houses on the edge of a town or city.

Further Information

Books to Read

Brownlie, Alison. *Jamaica* (Country Insights). Austin, TX: Raintree Steck-Vaughn, 1998.

Mayer, T. W. *The Caribbean and Its People* (People and Places). Austin, TX: Thomson Learning, 1995.

McKenley, Yvonne. *A Taste of the Caribbean*. Austin, TX: Raintree Steck-Vaughn, 1997.

Pluckrose, Henry. *Jamaica* (Picture a Country). Danbury, CT: Franklin Watts, 1998.

Sheean, Sean. *Jamaica* (Cultures of the World). Tarrytown, NY: Marshall Cavendish, 1993.

Useful Addresses

Jamaican Embassy
1520 New Hampshire Avenue
Washington, DC 20036
(202) 452-0660

Jamaican Tourist Board
866 Second Avenue
New York, NY 10017
(212) 688-7650

Index

All the numbers in **bold** refer to illustrations.